Events in the History of
Mission Santa Barbara and the United States

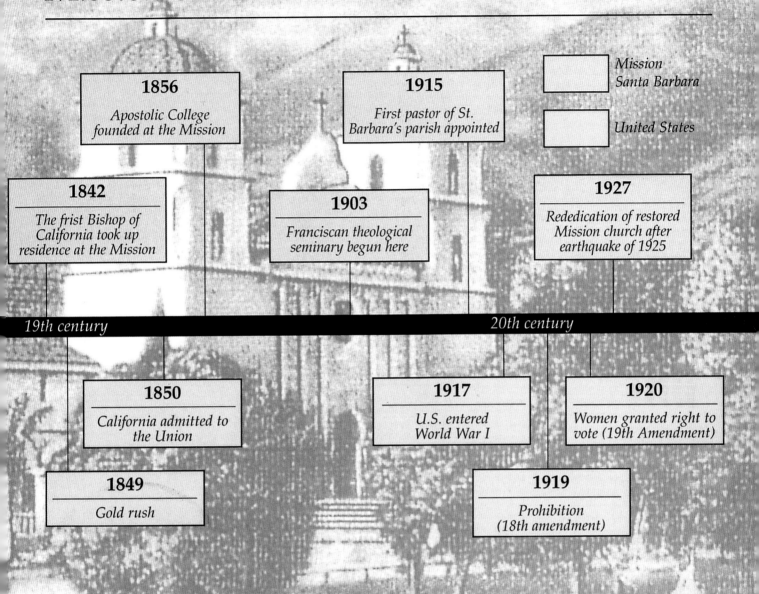

1856

Apostolic College founded at the Mission

1915

First pastor of St. Barbara's parish appointed

Mission Santa Barbara

United States

1842

The frist Bishop of California took up residence at the Mission

1903

Franciscan theological seminary begun here

1927

Rededication of restored Mission church after earthquake of 1925

19th century   20th century

1850

California admitted to the Union

1917

U.S. entered World War I

1920

Women granted right to vote (19th Amendment)

1849

Gold rush

1919

Prohibition (18th amendment)

Based on a text by Maynard Geiger, O.F.M., Ph.D

Mission *Queen of the Missions* Santa Barbara

Contents

Produced for the Franciscan Friars and the Serra Shop, Old Mission Santa Barbara
Santa Barbara, California

ISBN 1-56933-012-3 Printed in Korea
© CKI, Inc. BK-SS-002

INTRODUCTION

By Father Virgil Cordano, O.F.M.

For over two hundred years this mission has been blessed in serving the needs of differing people in a variety of ways. Like a queen surrounded by a royal court of kneeling hills, praying seas, protecting islands, red-tiled roofs, and trees and flowers of all colors, she has been many things over the years: a wellspring of Christian Indian life, a home for Franciscan friars, a seminary for aspirants to the Franciscan order, a school for the laity, a parish church, a place of spiritual renewal, and an archive-library rich in recorded memories of her noble past. Those who stand before her admire her mingling of Hispanic, Roman, Grecian and Moorish architecture. Those who walk through her doors contemplate her works of art and discover rest and hope in prayer.

We relate this glorious history in the following text and pictures. We are grateful for all that has come to us from the past, and accept the challenge to equal and, perhaps, surpass the achievements of those who served this Mission and from here, served others. May Mission Santa Barbara continue to treasure values that endure through all times and cultures so that whatever is true, noble, and beautiful may be within the reach of, and for the enjoyment of, all. May we, in continuity with the many people who, while under different flags, heard these same Missions bells, keep life an open road, reaching as far as the ends of the earth and as high as the sky above – as Junipero Serra wrote "always go forward and never turn back."

VISITING MISSION SANTA BARBARA

Your visit around the public areas of the Mission starts at the Gift Shop to the left of the Mission Church. Here, you may purchase tickets for the tour which starts at the entrance to the Museum. The Gift Shop also offers a wide range of books, postcards and souvenirs.

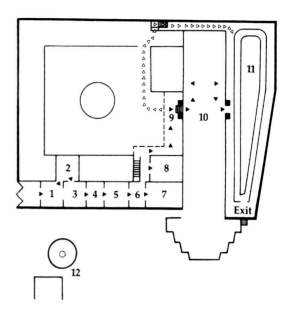

◁ *Route used if church services are being held*

Originally, the museum rooms were used as living quarters for the missionaries and guests. Now they contain a rich collection of historical artifacts, some of which date from the earliest mission period. The museum rooms and important areas are in the following sequence:

1. The Founding of Mission Santa Barbara
2. The Building Period and Oldest Known Photographs
3. A Missionary's Bedroom
4. Chumash Indian Art Room
5. Mission Trades
6. The First Bishop Of California
7. The Kitchen
8. Video and Early Mission Music Room
9. The Sacred Gardens: This was once a working area where many Indians learned trades. The workshops and some Indian living quarters were located in the surrounding buildings.
10. The Mission Church: Here are many examples of eighteenth-and nineteenth-century Mexican art. The two marble plaques on the floor identify the early missionaries and laymen buried in the crypt below.
11. The Cemetery: The skulls above the door indicate the cemetery, where approximately 4,000 Indians are buried. The vaults and mausoleums date from the 1850s to the present. The large mausoleum in the rear is used by the Franciscans.
12. The Fountain: This Moorish fountain was built in 1808. The long basin is a lavanderia, used by the Indian women to wash clothes.

ONE / THE HISTORY OF MISSION SANTA BARBARA

THE DISCOVERY, NAMING AND SETTLEMENT OF SANTA BARBARA

The coast, channel and islands of the Santa Barbara area were discovered by Juan Rodriguez Cabrillo, a Portuguese in the maritime service of Spain, in 1542. It was only in 1602, however, that the name Santa Barbara, was applied to the area. That year witnessed the return of a Spanish force, led by Sebastian Vicaino, accompanied by Carmelite friars. They entered the channel on December 3, the vigil of the Feast of St. Barbara, and gave her name to the body of water; this name was later applied to the presidio, mission, city and county of Santa Barbara.

But it would be many years before the name was brought ashore. Not until 1769 did European settlement of California take place. Jose de Galvez, inspector general of New Spain (Mexico) in the name of King Carlos III, ordered the occupation of New or Upper California to protect the king's southern domains against threatening Russian advances from the north.

The occupation, conquest and settlement of California was a co-operative enterprise on the party of State and Church. It was to be a peaceful conquest. Though military and political reasons occasioned it, the method was to be carried out in a Christian manner. Once occupied, California was to be Christianized and civilized through the use of the mission system, which had proven effective in other areas.

To advance this plan, Galvez invited the Franciscans then laboring in Lower (Baja) California to assume the spiritual and cultural burdens of the conquest. Fray Junipero Serra, the president of those missions, eagerly responded. The matter was proposed to the viceregal court in Mexico City, ruled by Viceroy Carolos de Croix, and to the College of San Fernando, whence the Franciscan missionaries came. The enterprise was approved. Four expeditions were readied, two by land, two by sea, and all

converged upon San Diego. There, on July 16, 1769, Father Serra raised the cross and founded the first mission. San Diego, therefore, is truly the cradle of Christianity and civilization in California.

ON TO SANTA BARBARA

Though a mission was planned for the Santa Barbara Channel early in the conquest, effective occupation occurred only in 1782, when California's ninth mission, San Buenaventura, was founded at Ventura, on March 31. Soon thereafter, Governor Felipe de Neve, Fray Junipero Serra and Captain Jose Francisco Ortetga set out with fifth soldiers and their families, and a few Indian servants, traveling along the beach to the area of present-day Santa Barbara. During a week's stay there, Neve chose the site for the presidio which was to guard the channel. For the time being, the presidio and mission were to be one until a new site nearby could be selected for the latter. With this understanding, Serra raised and blessed the cross, blessed the land and said Mass on April 21, 1782. Thus Santa Barbara came into formal existence.

SANTA BARBARA'S BIRTH CERTIFICATE

The original records of baptisms, marriages and burials commenced on the day of Santa Barbara's founding. Fray Serra himself inscribed the pertinent information on the initial pages of this invaluable volume, which is preserved in the Mission Archive. Bound in covers of soft leather, the leaves of durable watermarked paper are filled with specimens of beautiful handwriting and rich vital statistics. From that initial page, we give here in English translation the words which constitute the birth certificate of the Santa Barbara Mission:

"Burial Register which contains the entries of burials of those who died at this Mission and Royal Presidio of Santa Barbara, Virgin and Martyr, administered by the Reverend Missionary Fathers of the Apostolic College of the Propagation of the Faith of San Fernando in Mexico City, who belong to the Order of Our Holy Father, St. Francis, of the Observance, founded at the expense of and by order of the Catholic King of Spain and of the Indies, Carlos III (Whom may God prosper forever)in Upper California along the shores of the Channel of Santa Barbara, by the religious of the said college, begun on the third Sunday after Easter, and on the Patronage of the Most Holy Patriarch, St. Joseph, Spouse of Mary Most Holy, on April 21 in the year 1782, on which occasion I, the undersigned Fray Junipero Serra, President of these Missions among the said infidels of the said apostolic college and in its name, with holy water blessed the earth and a large cross which we raised and venerated. In a brush chapel I celebrated the holy sacrifice of the Mass, the first in this area and preached concerning the occasion. Because I had no companion, the Mass was a recited one and in place of the Te Deum, I terminated the ceremony with the Alabado. May it be for the greater glory of God, the spread of the holy Faith, and the good of souls. The first missionaries of this mission which for the time being is one with the presidio, will leave (for here) as soon as they are assigned. This book contains 192 useful leaves not counting the first and last which remains blank. As a witness thereunto, I have attached my name."

....Fray Junipero Serra

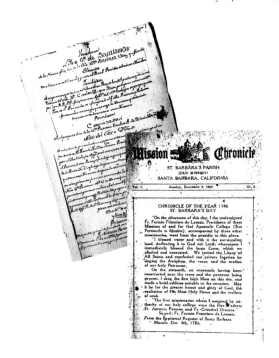

The original Mission Santa Barbara dedication statement by Fr. Lasuen and a translation that appeared in the Mission Chronicle.

SERRA'S PLANS FRUSTRATED

Serra actually believed that he had founded California's tenth mission that April morning – he would never have proclaimed it unless there had been official agreement with the governor on the matter, for no mission could be founded without government permission. However, Governor Neve had come to believe that the military should take precedence, with the missionaries limited to spiritual matters – contrary to the balance of Church and State which had overseen the establishment of previous mission settlements. After three weeks of waiting, Serra was told by Neve that he could not proceed with the mission until the presidio building was finished. Serra knew that this would take a long time. Because pressing business matters were awaiting him at Carmel and Monterey, the traveled north, biding his time. Meanwhile, the spiritual needs of the soldiers and settlers at Santa Barbara were taken care of by the missionaries at San Buenaventura, who visited the new outpost from time to time. Fray Serra paid two brief visits to Santa Barbara in the latter half of 1783, both times conferring the sacrament of confirmation in the presidio chapel. Governor Pedro Fages succeeded Neve in 1783. In the summer of 1784, he

Mission Santa Barbara

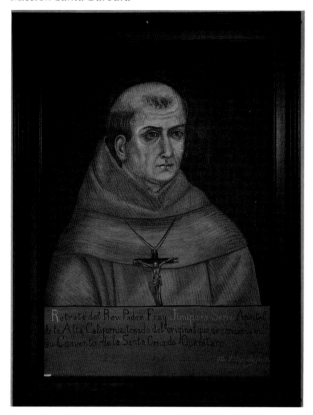

Padre Junipero Serra, O.F.M.

*A terracotta plaque commemorating the 1925
Santa Barbara earthquake.*

notified Serra that he could begin to establish Mission Santa Barbara, but Serra died at Mission San Carlos in Carmel on August 28 of that year, at the age of 71. The diminutive padre had ranged over a vast, strange, often hostile territory to establish an extraordinary series of Christian outposts. Neve preceded him in death by seven days on the desert of northern Mexico. Despite their differences, the two men had together brought the Cross and the Crown to channel shores, and founded Santa Barbara.

MISSION SANTA BARBARA FOUNDED

The official founding of Mission Santa Barbara would be left to Father Fermin Francisco de Lasuen, who succeeded Father Serra as President of the California Missions in 1785. The first mission he founded was that of Santa Barbara. He chose as the site the top of a rising slope of land which looked over the valley and channel – perhaps the most striking and commanding site of all the 21 missions. It was called Tanayan by the Indians and Pedregoso by the Spaniards; both words mean "Rocky Mound." The site was located about a mile and a half to the north-

east of the presidio. On that hill, where the present mission stands, Father Lasuen raised the cross and blessed it on December 4, 1786. He also started three registers, as Serra had done for the presidio. The latter were used only for the vital statistics of the non-Indian population, while the statistics of the Christian Indians were recorded in the mission registers.

Since Governor Fages had not arrived in time for the planting of the cross on December 4, another formal ceremony was held at the same place on December 16, on which occasion Mass was said by Lasuen, who also delivered a brief sermon. Though Fages considered December 16 the official datae of founding, the Franciscan missionaries of the mission period, as well as their successors today, have always considered and celebrated December 4 as the actual date of founding. Lasuen's formal entries of the facts of founding are very similar to those of Serra in 1782 and need not be repeated here. The president appointed Fathers Antonio Paterna and Cristobal Oramas as Santa Barbara missionaries. The former was a seasoned veteran, having been an Indian missionary in America since 1750 and a companion of Father Serra.

SPANISH AND INDIAN NAMES

Acalanes: Indian tribe
Adobe: sun-dried brick
Alabado: a hymn of praise
Alameda: shaded walk
Alamo: poplar tree
Alcatraz: pelican
Alisal: clump of alder or elderberry trees
Arroyo Grande: big creek
Asunción: feast of the Assumption
Atascadero: swampy ground
Atole: mush made of corn meal
Barranca: ravine
Bellota: acorn
Blanco: white
Bodega: cellar, storeroom
Brea: pitch, tar
Buena Vista: beautiful view
Calabazas: pumpkins
Calaveras: skulls
Carpinteria: carpenter shop
Cayucos: canoes
Cazadero: hunting grounds
Conejo: rabbit
Contra Costa: opposite coast
Corral de Piedra: stone or rock fence
Crucero: cross bearer
Del Mar: of or at the sea
Del Monte: of or at the mountain
Del Rey: of or from the king
Del Sur: of or from the south
Descanso: rest or repose
Dios: God
Doctrina: instruction
Dolores: sorrows
Don: the Spanish title for a gentleman
Do_a: a married lady
Dos Palos: two trees
Dos Pueblos: two towns
El Cajón: box
El Camino Real: king's highway
El Céntro: center
El Molino: mill
El Monte: mountain, forest
El Paseo: walk
El Toro: bull
Embarcadero: place of departure
Encino: evergreen oak
Ensenada: cover, small bay
Escondido: hidden
Fiesta: feast
Fray: Friar, brother
Fresno: ash tree
Frijoles: beans
Garbanzos: peas
Gaviota: sea gull
Goleta: schooner
Hermosa: beautiful
Horno: oven

Hornitos: little ovens
Islay: wild cherry
Jolón: valley of dead trees (Indian)
Junípero: juniper
La Ca_ada: valley, canyon, glen
La Honda: deep (water)
La Mesa: table-land
La Mirada: view
La Piedra: stone
La Playa: beach
La Puente: bridge
Las Cruces: crosses
Los Alamos: cottonwoods, poplar trees
Los Altos: heights
Los Gatos: cats
Los Ojitos: little springs
Los Olivos: olive trees
Madre: mother
Mano: hand, small grinding stone
Manteca: lard, fat
Manzana: apple
Mayordomo: superintendent, majordomo
Mesa Grande: big table-land
Metate: a curved stone for grinding maize
Mezcla: a hard plaster also used for a floor surface
Milpitas: small truck gardens
Modesto: modest
Montecito: small mountain or forest
Monterey: king's mountain
Morro: headland
Nacimiento: birth, origin
Naranjo: orange tree
Nogales: walnut trees
Nopal: prickly pear tree
Nuestro: our
Nuevo: new
Ojai: moon (Indian)
Oro Grande: coarse gold
Padre: father
Pájaro: bird
Palo Alto: tall tree
Palo Verde: green tree
Paraíso: paradise
Paso de Robles: oak pass
Patio: open court
Pescadero: fishing place
Petaluma: low hills
Piedra Blanca: white stone
Pinole: corn meal
Plaza: public square
Potrero: pasture
Pozo: well
Pozole: heavy soup with meat, vegetables and grain
Presidio: garrison of soldiers
Pueblo: town, village
Puente: bridge
Pulga: flea
Punta Gordia: big point

Ranchería: hamlet, cluster of huts
Rebozo: muffler, shawl
Redondo: round
Rincón: corner
Rodel: round-up of cattle
Sacramento: Sacrament
Salinas: salt pits
San Andrés: St. Andrew
San Bernardino: St. Bernardine (Franciscan)
San Buenaventura: St. Boneventure (Franciscan)
San Diego: St. Didacus (Franciscan)
San Fernando Rey: St. Ferdinand, King of Spain
San Francisco: St. Francis
San Gabriel: St. Gabriel
San Jacinto: St. Hyacinth
San Joaquin: St. Joachim
San José: St. Joseph
San Juan Bautista: St. John the Baptist
San Juan Capistrano: St. John Capistrano (Franciscan)
San Luis Obispo: St. Louis, the Bishop (Franciscan)
San Luis Rey: St. Louis, King of France
San Marcos: St. Mark
San Mateo: St. Matthew
San Miguel: St. Michael
San Pablo: St. Paul
San Pascual: St. Paschal (Franciscan)
San Pedro: St. Peter
San Quintin: St. Quentin
San Rafael: St. Raphael
San Simeón: St. Simeon
Santa Ana: St. Anne
Santa Barbara: St. Barbara
Santa Catalina: St. Catherine
Santa Clara: St. Clare
Santa Cruz: Holy Cross
Santa Inés: St. Agnes
Santa Isabel: St. Elizabeth
Santa Lucia: St. Lucy
Santa Margarita: St. Margaret
Santa Maria: Holy Mary
Sauzalito: small clumps of willows
Siesta: afternoon nap
Soledad: solitude
Tejón: badger
Temescal: sweat bath (Indian)
Tiburón: shark
Tortilla: thin cornmeal cake
Tres Pinos: three pine trees
Valle Vista: valley view
Vaquero: cowboy
Wawona: big tree (Indian)
Yosémite: grizzly bear (Indian)
Zaguán: entrance hall
Zanja: ditch, trench

THE INDIANS OF SANTA BARBARA

The Indians of the present coastal counties of Ventura, Santa Barbara and San Luis Obispo belonged to the Chumash tribe, with a common language but varied dialects. This was the most thickly settled area of native of native California, with about 15,000 natives living in Chumash territory. Of all the Indians who came under Spanish rule between San Diego and San Francisco after 1769, those of the Santa Barbara Channel area were the most numerous and most culturally advanced, and probably the best documented. The Chumash were hunters and gatherers, with tools and weapons made of stone, shell, wood and bone. The arrival of the Spanish brought about a meeting of Stone Age and advanced Iron Age cultures, an encounter between drastically different societies.

The early Spaniards noted that the Chumash had a lively temperament and an industrious disposition. Early Spanish accounts describe the natives as generally affable, agile and clever. They lived in large, well-laid-out villages of semi-sperical thatched huts, some of great size. Though disputes among villages were common, the Indians were friendly and hospitable towards the Spanish. The area from Rincon (just south of Carpinteria) to Dos Pueblos (north of Santa Barbara) contained the most populous villages. Each village had a chief who ruled for life. Santa Barbara, then called Siujtu, was ruled by the chief Yanonali and contained about five hundred inhabitants. The largest cluster of villages, with perhaps 1,500 people, surrounded the Goleta slough.

The Chumash men generally went about entirely naked, sometimes wearing cloaks made of animal skins. The women wore animal-skin-skirts and adorned themselves with trinkets of sea shells and colorful stones. They were excellent dancers and wore plumage, painting their bodies for war and the dance. The Indians performed frequently for the early Spanish expeditions, the dancers accompanied

Chumash Indian Rafael Solares in dance costume circa 1878. The photograph was taken by Leon de Cessac, a French anthropologist, during his travels in California.

by flutes, rattles and singing that was occasionally unpleasant to European ears, although the Spanish appreciated the overall harmony and unison of song and dance.

Fully developed Chumash villages contained a temescal, a recreation area and a cemetery. The temescal, which translates as "place of sweat baths," was a partly subterranean structure of poles and earth, a sort of sauna heated by a fire. After descending into it by ladder, people would sit for some time, sweating profusely, then climb out, jump into the surf and bathe. The recreation area was a smooth, level place where games were played. Located close to the village, the cemetery held graves marked by painted poles planted in the ground to which were attached objects belonging to the deceased, such as skirts, baskets, shell beads and other personal possessions.

Shrines consisting of poles, painted and decorated with plumage, were placed near a village. Indians would leave offerings at these sites, which the Spanish called adoratories. In the Santa Barbara area, the Indians called their god Shup, in whose honor they scattered seeds and bird feathers during the religious ceremonies, as an act of gratitude. When an Indian died, the body was carried to a special place, where a watch was kept over it during the night. The burial ceremony took place about a large fire at daybreak, and included ritual tobacco smoking, sorrowful song and presentation of beads to the chief mourner. The Chumash were buried in a fetal position. Some objects were placed in the grave, some atop it.

The Chumash skillfully plied the channel with their long, well-fashioned canoes, which they used for fishing as well as bartering with the natives of the Channel Islands. The Chumash were skilled at native crafts, which included basket weaving and woodworking. The Spanish admired their patterned basketware, wooden plates and bowls, and flint-hewn mortars and crocks made of black stone, sometimes inlaid with mother of pearl. The Chumash were exceptional in that they slept in high bedsteads, with reed mats as mattresses. The natives' dexterity and energy were to serve the Mission well.

Once settled among the Indians, the small Spanish community set about converting these native Americans to a Christian, European way of life. Father Serra and other Spaniards realized that, united, the Chumash could crush an isolated garrison and cut colonial California in two. Accordingly, the newcomers took pains not to provoke the natives, who never organized their forces. Governor Neve believed the establishment of missions in the area could cause grave trouble if the missionaries tried to make the Indians work or leave their native villages to live at the mission. He declared Indian villages generally off limits for Spanish soldiers, and forbade violence toward the Chumash. When Neve finally authorized the founding of Mission Santa Barbara, after his promotion to Commandant of the Interior

Above: A Chumash couple at the Mission Santa Barbara in 1882. Left: Juan Justo, one of the last surviving full blooded Chumash. The famous Santa Barbara anthropologist, John Harrington, worked extensively with Justo recording oral histories.

Provinces, he gave careful orders to Governor Fages regarding the natives:

"I consent that it be effected in such a way as not to offend the Indians. You will see to it that they are treated with the greatest gentleness and sweetness lest this foundation be repugnant to them. You will carefully avoid giving them the least occasion for pain."

The caution exercised by the Spanish in dealing with the Indians permitted peaceful colonization, largely avoiding the violent clashes that could easily have resulted from the great disparity in the sizes and cultures of the two populations. Nevertheless, the coming of the white man marked the beginning of the end for the Chumash, who had almost disappeared by the end of the following half-century of foreign disruption and disease, and natural attrition.

THE MISSION FLOURISHES (1787 – 1828)

During the early period of their existence, missions were quite crude in structure and appearance. Their development into full-grown institutions often took years. Santa Barbara was no different in this respect. The first buildings were log cabins whose crevices were filled with mud and stones, who floors were bare earth and whose roofs were of pressed earth and sacate grass. At Santa Barbara the padres lived at the presidio until building at the mission could be undertaken after the spring rains of 1787. The missionaries' new residence measured 44 feet by 13 feet 9 inches, while the first chapel measured 38 feet 6 inches by 13 feet 9 inches. Among the first buildings were also a kitchen, granary and servants' rooms. Tile began to be used as roof covering in 1788. Mission Santa Barbara was built in such a way that when completed it formed a quadrangle. The first quadrangle was finished in 1795. After that, a second one, adjoining it, was begun.

Upper: Padres on Mission Dam, Santa Barbara Botanic Gardens Lower: This photograph of the Misson shows the reservoir used by the Franciscan community prior to 1900.

VARIOUS CHURCH STRUCTURES

In 1789, a new church structure was begun at the mission to serve the needs of the growing congregation. Made of adobe, it measured 82 feet by 16 feet 6 inches. This was followed by a third church, also of adobe, but more elaborate, with six side chapels. This church, which was finished by Father Estevan Tapis in 1794, measured 123 feet by 25 feet. It stood until the earthquake of 1812, when it was severely damaged. The padres then decided to build of more durable stone, of which there was an abundance in the immediate neighborhood. Work did not begin until 1815 (the repaired adobe being used meanwhile) and was completed in 1820.

This church – the one in use today – was dedicated on September 10, 1820, in a colorful celebration attended by Governor Pablo Sola. The builders were Fathers Antonio Ripoll and Francisco Suner. The new structure measured 161 feet by 27 feet and 42 feet in height. The single tower rose to a height of 87 feet (the second tower was added in the years 1831-

1833). The façade of the church is an adaptation of a Roman temple design found in an illustrated volume by Vitruvius Polion, a famous architect of the Augustan period. The Mission reflects other influences as well, visible, for example, in the splayed Moorish windows that indent the thick masonry walls.

The front arcade of Roman arches, finished in 1811, originally featured sixteen arches, later expanded to eighteen. The original tile walk of the corridor is still in place. The mission living quarters were of one story with a flat roof, called an azotea; above this was raised a roof of tile upon columns that gave the "second story" the appearance of an open attic. In the latter part of the nineteenth century, this was ungraded into the substantial second story visible today. For further information, see the "Art and Architecture" chapter.

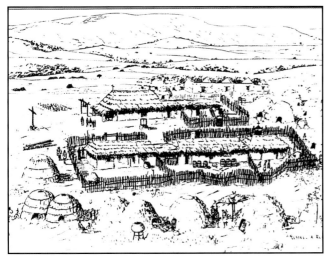

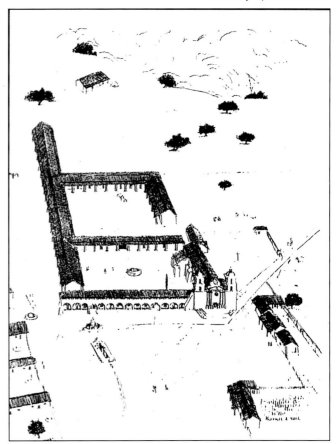

These drawings by Russell A. Ruiz show the Mission Santa Barbara in three early stages. Upper left: 1787; lower left: 1812; above: 1833.

THE CHRISTIAN INDIAN VILLAGE

The first Indian converts to Christianity who began to live at the mission built their huts there after their native fashion. In 1798 a new type of home appeared; adobe houses with tile roofs. These were built adjoining each other and back to back along straight streets whose intersections crossed at right angles. The area set aside for this Christian Indian village measured about 350 by 700 feet. Within eight years, 252 individual homes were built. This village, surrounded by a wall, existed immediately west of the mission living quarters and the front fountain. It was Santa Barbara's first housing project.

WATER AND IRRIGATION

One of the prime requisites of every mission was, of course, water in sufficient quantity to maintain its inhabitants and to cultivate its fields. Mission Santa Barbara was located with the intent that Rio Pedregoso (Mission Creek) would serve that pur-

pose. Two dams were built to impound the waters of this creek and its Rattlesnake Canyon tributary. Mission Dam, containing the waters of Mission Creek, is today well preserved, and indicated by an historical marker in the Botanic Gardens. Water was carried to the mission by gravity flow through stone aqueducts, large sections of which still exist. These converged northeast of the mission where there was a distribution system consisting of a storage reservoir, settling tank, and a second reservoir which even today forms a part of the Santa Barbara water system. The reservoir was built in 1806; the dam in 1807. The beautiful Moorish fountain and Indian community wash basin, a part of the water system, was constructed in 1808. Ruins of the reservoir and other buildings, such as the pottery works, may be seen in Mission Historical Park, northeast of the mission along Alameda Padre Serra and Los Olivos Street, this side of Mission Canyon Bridge. From here, aqueducts ran behind, along and to the south of the mission; the southern aqueduct was used to irrigate the mission garden and may still be seen in Mission Park, across from the east tower.

AGRICULTURE AND STOCK RAISING

The principal industrial occupations at Mission Santa Barbara, as well as at other missions, were agriculture and stock raising. In the beginning, a new mission was supplied with seeds, a few cattle and other animals, and was aided for some years by existing,more prosperous missions. Each mission was supposed to become self-sustaining in the matter of food and clothing in the course of time. The principal crops were wheat, maize, barley, beans and chick-peas. Planting began at Santa Barbara during the first year. It should be kept in mind that these Indians, when discovered, were pre-agricultural, and so had to be taught farming. Prior to that, they had lived on fish from the adjacent Pacific and from seeds and wild animals on land. Even after agriculture was introduced, the natives continued to supplement their food supply with the foods of their pre-Christian state. The padres, together with a soldier majordomo who was in charge of the farm under their supervision and a few Christian Indians brought from Lower California, had to encourage and train the local Indians in a type of work to which they had not been accustomed. What was produced was stored away for common use and rationed, but generously bestowed according to individual needs.

Mission Santa Barbara started with 80 head of cattle, 27 sheep, 87 goats, 32 horses and 9 mules. Mission livestock herds peaked in 1814, when the total number of animals on the mission lands amounted to 16,598 including sheep, cattle, horses, mules, goats and pigs. These animals were kept at ranchos established over a large area by the friars, mainly on Indian lands. Of the 64 bushels of grain planted the first year, the mission fields yielded 265 bushels. The banner year for production was 1821, when 12,820 bushels were harvested. Agriculture was also carried on in outlying areas as well as at the Mission. At Dos Pueblos, Sagspileel (Goleta) and San Estevan, wheat was grown. Corn and beans were grown at San Jose, the Sauzal (near Hope Ranch) and Arroyo del Burro.

DEALING WITH THE INDIANS

The padres achieved the difficult task of attracting the Indians by gifts and kindness, and by persuading them to accept Christianity and the

Upper: This engraving of the Mission was executed in 1833. Lower: An early cobbler.

European way of life. The missionaries had to learn the native language. They taught Spanish to the brighter boys and young men, who became interpreters. Once the Indian was baptized, often after prolonged instruction and living at the mission for a period, he was expected to reside in the Christian Indian village at the Mission and follow the manner of life lived there. The padres remained the guides, instructors, overseers and defenders of the Indians. Christianized Indians were allowed liberal vacations to visit their relatives and former villages. This policy gave the Christian Indians a change as well as attracting non-Christian Indians to the Mission.

The restored padres' kitchen, now on display in the Mission Museum, shows typical indoor cooking facilities of the early 1800s. The wall on the left is the original adobe.

Besides Sundays, there were many church festivals during the year, when all labor ceased. At sunrise a bell called the Indians to church. There one of the padres said Mass, attended by the Indians, while the other padres recited with them the principal Christian prayers and went over with them elements of the Christian doctrine. Hence this exercise was known as the doctrina. Breakfast followed, after which work was apportioned. The Indians reassembled for their noon meal and a siesta, which was followed by a couple hours of work in the afternoon. After another church gathering in the evening came supper, and a time for games and leisure. Girls and unmarried women slept in special quarters, called the monjerio, under the supervision of a Spanish matron. Between the years 1786 and 1846, the padres assisted at 4,715 baptisms, 1,397 marriages and 3,997 burials in Santa Barbara and its environs. The largest number of Indians living at the Mission at any single time was in 1803, when they numbered 1,792.

GENERAL PICTURE OF MISSION LIFE

The Franciscan padres' purpose at the missions was primarily spiritual: instructing and converting the Indians and maintaining them in the observance of Christian life. They clearly saw, however, that their efforts in this regard could not be accomplished without assuming the economic, social and cultural burdens of mission life as an indispensable means to their primary end. They were first of all missionaries of their faith, but at the same time they were agents of the Spanish realm, producing not only Christians but also useful citizens of the empire. They acted as administrators over the mission, its lands and movable goods, in the name of the Indians. No part of a mission was ever Franciscan property. The salaries that were given to the missionaries were not even sent to California, but were deposited at San Fernando College in Mexico, when they were spent for special needs of the missions, often for cloth to

Right (upper): Front view of Mission.
Right (lower): A typical missionary's
bedroom of the early 1800s. The wooden
cabinet is one of the oldest pieces of furni-
ture in the Mission.

clothe the Indians. The thousand pesos given to each mission at its founding was likewise spent in Mexico for the mission's initial needs. The King of Spain donated a large and a small bell. The money spent on a mission came from the Pious Fund of the Californias, a fund gathered by the Jesuit missionaries of Lower California before they were expelled by the Spanish king in 1767.

The mission records, which are abundant, reveal that life at a mission such as Santa Barbara was an industrious one for the two missionaries stationed there. They had to plan the buildings, manage the farms, supervise the livestock, keep accounts, give religious instructions, keep records (and they were kept meticulously), learn the language and administer the sacraments. They had helpers, it is true, in the jajordomo who took care of the economic side of the mission under their direction. The Spanish matron guided the women. There were some Christian Indian helpers, and a corporal and five soldiers guarded the mission and kept order. Later, stonemasons and builders from Mexico were supplied to help in constructing the more imposing edifices. It has been estimated that some fifty trades were taught at the mission, among them farming and care of cattle, shoemaking and saddlemaking, carpentry and blacksmithing, tile making and adobe manufacturing, stone cutting, spinning and weaving, making of soap and candles, etc. Through dramatics such as the annual Christmas play, and through music and singing, the Indian was brought into closer touch with Christian and European tradition. Father Narciso Duran (who died in 1846) was the man at Santa Barbara most gifted in music. During ten years of work, he forged an accomplished band of Indian musicians, which contributed greatly to church services and celebrations.

The padre in charge of the mission wrote to the president of the missions yearly, giving a report of progress at the mission and making requests for things he needed. In turn, the president communicated these needs to Mexico. Thus, year after year until 1811, the Mission church became beautified with statues, paintings, vestments and other church goods, many of which remain to this day. Statues on the reredos behind the main altar and painting along the walls attest to the padres' endeavors to obtain pieces of art of no mean value. The various feasts of the Church, such as Christmas and Epiphany, Holy Week and Corpus Christi, were observed with becoming splendor.

SECULARIZATION AND REVIVAL FROM 1828 TO THE PRESENT

DISSOLUTION OF THE MISSION SYSTEM

The missionaries of Hispanic California hoped that one day they would be able to turn these missions over to a bishop and depart for new mission fields. But that time never came. Before such an event happened, the missions were secularized, then confiscated, and the mission period came to an end. The decline and dissolution of the mission system through secularization and confiscation is a long, sad and complicated story. In a work as brief at this, we can state only certain facts that highlight this tragic demise. The original meaning of secularization was that Indian missions were to be transferred from the jurisdiction of missionaries of religious orders into the hands of a bishop who would administer them through his "secular" or diocesan priests. Theoretically, Indian missions were to be handed over to such new jurisdiction after a period of ten years. This latter law was largely inoperative because in many cases, adequate personnel for diocesan jurisdiction were not available.

The ten years allowed before the transition was an insufficient amount of time to acculturate the native Indian population of European civilization. As a matter of fact, the seventy years of the California mission period were not enough to achieve it. The mission system was doomed by both external and internal factors. The new republican ideals of independent Mexico, the desire of colonists for mission lands and the gain envisioned by private individuals were the principal external factors sounding the death knell of the mission system. Internally, the Indians were dying faster than they were born, though in 1831 there were still 18,315 Indians living in the twenty-one missions. By 1828 almost all of the old Indian villages in the Santa Barbara area had ceased to exist. Missionization of the area's surviving Indians had largely been accomplished, but their population had decreased so much that the end of the first mission phase was on the horizon. In any

The Santa Ynez mountains tower over Mission Santa Barbara in this late nineteenth century photograph.

event, it is inconceivable that the mission system would have continued as in the past once California became American territory, for the system presupposed a close union of Church and State.

SECULARIZATION AND CONFISCATION

In 1826, Governor Echeandia, without authorization, issued a law concerning partial secularization of the missions and emancipation of the Indians. In 1827, Mexico passed a law banishing from its dominions all Spaniards, which included most of the California missionaries. Both laws remained largely inoperative because they were impractical with regard to California. In 1833, and 1834, Mexico passed laws ordering secularization and in the latter year made it mandatory within four months. The new governor, Jose Figueroa, had no choice but to act in enforcing the law, following a more sensible policy of gradual secularization and emancipation. Within two years, lay administrators were appointed over the temporal affairs of the twenty-one missions. The majority were incompetent and/or greedy, so that when William Hartnell was appointed in 1839 as inspector of the missions and saw what damage had taken place, he proposed remedial measures. But opposition to his reform was so strong that he resigned. Governor Micheltorena restored the missions to the Franciscans in 1843, but by that time they were so fragmented that they could not be revived. In 1845, Governor Pio Pico authorized the rental and/or sale of the missions.

EARTHQUAKE!
JUNE 19, 1925

"On the morning of the 1925 earthquake, I was attending a High Mass in the Mission church. We students were singing upstairs in the choir. All of a sudden there came a strong upward movement. Then it moved from one side to the other. You could see the statues in the altarpiece niches turning! I ran into the sacred garden and, looking back, I could see one of the towers falling. The little pond in the center of the garden was moving from side to side, and the water was splashing out. There was a father, Geronimo Piazzo, who was saying mass at the little altar at the back of the church. As the people who were attending the mass started to rush out of the church, he said, 'Stop, stop, stop! Kneel down – we'll first have a blessing: Lord help us all...' And so he said a short prayer, and then he told them, 'All right, now go'. And they left, and within the space of that benediction, the big pieces of the front of the church had come down, and there were loads of bricks and stones ...these people would have been hit, maybe even killed by some of these large pieces! Just that short moment, maybe ten or twenty seconds, was enough to save them. Luckily, nobody was hurt at the old Mission. After the earthquake, we had no place for eating or sleeping, the walls were cracking. We had to live outside, sleep on little cots, have our meals outside, and the Mass there, too, with the altar under a canopy. The aftershocks kept us wondering what was going to happen next."

– Fr Alfred Boeddeker, O.F.M.
Mission Santa Barbara, July, 1986

Above: Rev. Zephrin Engelhardt, left, surveys earthquake damage with Rev. Augustine Hobrecht. Engelhardt was well known as a historian at the Mission, and Hobrecht was instrumental in rebuilding the Mission after the 1925 earthquake.

A drawing of the Mission made in 1865 by Edward Vischer. Fr. Rubio, president of the California missions, autographed it.

The Mission Santa Barbara in 1890, by Santa Barbara photographer N.H. Reed.

THE STATUS OF MISSION SANTA BARBARA

When the Missions were secularized, the church, cemetery and a few living rooms were left to the padres, whose labors from then on were largely confined to spiritual ministrations. In 1834, when Fathers Antonio Jimeno and Narciso Duran were missionaries of Santa Barbara, an inventory was drawn up and it was found that the property value of the mission, together with its ranchos and movable goods, was considered to be worth $113,960 and that its debts were $1,000. Because of the decline of the mission property under lay administrators, Inspector Hartnell asked Father Duran in 1839 to serve as administrator. However, the padre consented only to be the church director, not the temporal administrator.

When Mission Santa Barbara was leased to the highest bidders in 1845, it came into the hands of Nicholas A. Den and Daniel Hill for a period of nine years. They agreed to pay its debt and $1,200 in rent. The mission was finally sold to Den for $7,500, despite contrary orders from Mexico. This sale excluded lands claimed by the remaining Indians and the mission church. Den was to provide for the missionaries and the upkeep of divine service. Father Duran, the greatest Franciscan figure of the missions in the period of their decline, died in 1846. He lived to see the death and burial of what Serra had inaugurated sixty-four years before. Duran remained to the last the defender of the Indians.

CALIFORNIA'S FIRST BISHOP

Santa Barbara was signally honored by the presence of California's first bishop here between 1841 and 1846. This was Fray Francisco Garcia Diego, a former missionary, who had his headquarters in the mission, living quarters and his pro-cathedral (a cathedral located in a parish church) in the mission church. Bishop Diego was welcomed here in an enthusiastic and colorful demonstration. He opened the first theological seminary at Mission Santa Ines in 1844 and planned further institutions in Santa Barbara, but his plans were thwarted when President Santa Ana of Mexico confiscated the Pious Fund on which the California missions depended. Bishop Diego died in April 1846, and was buried in the sanctuary of Mission Santa Barbara on the Gospel side.

THE MISSION ASSUMES NEW ACTIVITIES

The late 1840s witnessed the Gold Rush and a great wave of American immigration. In 1850, California entered the United States Union. With the mission period ended, the Indians scattered or dead and the Stars and Stripes flying over Santa Barbara, the Franciscans decided on a new venture. The few remaining in California chose to establish an apostolic college, such as San Fernando in Mexico had been, a missionary center for California. They established this new college in Santa Barbara, not at the mission but at new quarters in the pueblo, on

The Mission Church interior in 1913.

The Mission Church interior in 1880.

the Den property at State and Figueroa Streets.

The college was officially opened on July 23, 1854, and the first novices to the Order in California received. Bishop Tadeo Amat, the new bishop of Monterey, chose Mission Santa Barbara as his cathedral and residence but after a short while considered it impractical. He requested the Franciscans to exchange their property in town for the old Mission, to which they consequently returned in 1856, continuing their apostolic college activities there until 1885. During that time a few priests were ordained and some brothers entered the Order, but the institution did not prosper by reason of an insufficient number of candidates and inadequate resources. Between the years 1868 and 1877, these Franciscans of the Apostolic College (called Our Lady of Sorrows) conducted at the Mission a boys' college (high school and junior college) called the Colegio Franciscano which also failed to mature into a lasting institution. Father Jose Maria Romo, who succeeded in office the aging and beloved Fray Jose Maria Gonzalez Rubio, made many needful repairs in the church and monastery during the years 1871 and 1874.

The impoverished Mission had come to the end of its second phase of activity, unsuccessful in its ventures. Its members harbored the thought of disbanding, which would have meant the end of Franciscanism in Santa Barbara, or of giving up an independent existence and joining an American province in order to give the Mission new life and purpose. The latter plan was adopted. Rome was consulted on the matter. It was adjudged best to make the Mission a house of the nearest Franciscan province, whose headquarters happened to be in St. Louis, Missouri. Thus the mission in 1885 became a part of the Province of the Sacred Heart. New friars were sent and activity expanded from the rejuvenated Mission along the Pacific slope until 1896, when the new Franciscan houses of the west were formed into a commissariat, or western division of the eastern province. In 1915, it was judged in Rome that there was a sufficient number of Franciscans in the west with the requisite number of friaries to make them an independent province. In January 1916, the first Father Provincial of the new province – Santa Barbara's Province – was installed at Mission Santa Barbara, though headquarters were moved to the Bay area. The Mission, however, always was and always will be the historic link between old mission days and the modern era.

NEW SEMINARY FOUNDED

In 1896, Fr. Peter Wallischeck arrived at Mission Santa Barbara to begin a junior seminary for aspirants to the Franciscan priesthood. This temporary seminary opened its doors at the old Mission in September 1896. It continued its existence here until 1901, when the new St. Anthony's Seminary was completed. This seminary, in augmented form, stands today to the northwest of the mission and adjoining it. Here aspirants complete their high school studies on the way to the priesthood. The college department was at Mission San Luis Rey. The four-year school of professional theology, which began at the mission in 1903, continued at Mission Santa Barbara until June 1968, when it was moved to Berkeley.

THE MISSION IN RUINS

A disastrous earthquake visited Santa Barbara on the morning of June 29, 1925, which did not spare the old Mission. The severest damage was wrought to the towers and façade of the church and to the front wing of the living quarters. It devolved upon Fr. Augustine Hobrecht, then superior, to restore and beautify the mission to its former splendor.

The restoration involved not only careful engineering but a scrupulous respect for the mission's history and architecture. The financial problem was even greater than the architectural one. A committee of prominent citizens was formed and the entire State of California was aroused. The cost of repair and restoration came close to $400,000, about half of which was raised by public subscription.

The façade and towers were constructed as they were before, and the church walls and roof strengthened, while the interior of the church was entirely done over, with a new reredos (painted canvas altarpiece), new altars and a newly painted interior based on the old. This restored church was solemnly consecrated on December 3, 1927, by Bishop John J. Cantwell of Los Angeles. The living quarters of the mission were reinforced with concrete and steel, thus being made safer against future tremors.

CONTINUED RESTORATION

Twenty-three years after its restoration, the sad news was conveyed to the padres that the towers and façade would have to be torn down, their foundations strengthened, and the entire front rebuilt with sturdier material. Technically, there had occurred a reaction between the alkalies and the aggregates in the cement. Cracks and fissures had appeared throughout the front of the structure, making it unsafe for public use. No blame was attached to the professionals who rebuilt the mission in 1925-1927, for what had happened was then beyond their control. Dismantling began in the middle of 1950, and the rebuilding was finished by August, 1953. The cost was over $300,000. More than half this cost was borne by the Fleischmann Foundation. The new façade was dedicated on December 4, 1953, by

James Francis Cardinal McIntyre, Archbishop of Los Angeles. The towers and façade are now well tied in to the rest of the church, with deep, sturdy foundations. They are of concrete reinforced with steel and have a stone facing more durable than the earlier stone. Towers and façade have the same dimensions and form as in the early days.

MISSION EXPANSION

In 1956, a new building program was initiated at the mission with the construction of two additional quadrangles, one of these replacing a quadrangle of mission days. At once a restoration and the realization of a practical need, the new area served as the quarters of the theological seminary. This new plant was dedicated on April 21, 1958. Father Noel Moholy, O.F.M., was the executive-director of the construction. The entire cost was borne by the Fleischmann Foundation. Thus the mission is now composed of three distinct quadrangles, or patios, all built in the original mission style.

The newest addition to the mission is the Archive-Library added to the west wing, replacing a wing built in 1905. This archive-library, completed in 1969, protects and preserves the scholarly resources of the Mission. This modern commodious facility gives scholars and writers access to the Mission's important collections of old and rare documents and books of the Hispanic period and mission activity in California.

SANTA BARBARA, QUEEN OF THE MISSIONS

Mission Santa Barbara is many things: a parish, a museum, an archive library, as well as a center of tourism. Its doors are open most days of the year, it activities are many and varied. Over 150,000 people come to its portals from every part of the world each year, the mission being considered Santa Barbara's chief cultural and historical attraction. These visitors are shown the museum rooms, cloister gardens, the church and the cemetery, with their priceless works of art, documents and varied artifacts, and the graves of the historic dead. Here the history and flavor the Mission period become vivid and compelling.

Mission Santa Barbara has for many years been called "Queen of the Missions." This title was

Above: The consecration of the restored Mission Santa Barbara on December 3, 1927. Bishop John J. Cantwell performed the service. Right: The Mission facade under reconstruction 1925-1927. Lower Right: Mass was said outside during the restoration of the Mission.

sponsored by none other than the famous historian of the missions, Father Zephyrin Engelhardt, O.F.M. The very location of the Mission, situated high on its hill, with the backdrop of the Santa Ynez Mission Ridge to the right, the Mesa to the left, and the sloping plain that runs from its feet straight down to the sea, gives it the look of a queen seated on her throne, from which she rules over the land. The Mission's commanding position and grand proportions, graceful lines and soft, blending colors all reinforce the title of "Queen." At her feet rests her empire, this beautiful city adorned with great beauty of architecture and flora, whose people honor her. Millions have come here from afar to do her reverence. The protecting islands, the placid and majestic sea, the enveloping hills and mountains form a perpetual bodyguard, colorfully costumed. It is a realm that any ruler would be glad to govern and proud to call her own. There is grace here rather than might, and charm rather than mass, warmth rather than strength. For all these reasons, the title "Queen of the Missions" has been bestowed upon her.

The story of the mission may be read in greater detail in Mission Santa Barbara (1782-1965) by Maynard Geiger, O.F.M., illustrated, 285 pages, $9.95, obtainable from the Serra Shop, Mission Santa Barbara.

TWO / ART AND ARCHITECTURE AT MISSION SANTA BARBARA

Placed as it is against a background of towering mountains, Mission Santa Barbara has undoubtedly the most dramatic location of any of the missions in California. The drama of the setting is now matched by the distinction of the architecture, but what one sees is the fourth church that has stood on this site. The first, built in 1787, was a simple structure of upright logs sealed with mud, with a roof of thatch; the following year it was lengthened in adobe and roofed with tile. That in turn was replaced by an adobe church in 1789. A more monumental and ambitious church of adobe was completed in 1794. It boasted six side chapels, opening into the nave as well as a brick, and then stone, portico in front. Its interior decorations were painted by padre Esteban Tapis and elicited the admiration of Padre Presidente Lasuen who judged the work of higher quality than what they had received from Mexico. This church, little by little, was furnished by statuary, painting and other equipment needed for the holy ceremonies. A painted canvass reredos, or altarpiece, was received from Mexico in 1806.

In 1809, the front row of rooms of the Fathers' dwelling was added in stone, and a stone arcade was placed in front two years later. This front wing of the quadrangle had a flat terrace roof with a parapet.

In 1812, a terrible earthquake hit the coast of California and the Mission was severely damaged. Repairs were made, but eventually a new church, this time in the local sandstone, was begun in 1815 and completed in 1820. It appears to have been constructed with the previous church still inside it, an exceptional but not unique process. Jose Antonio Ramirez who had built and designed the church at Mission San Luis Rey, was the master mason and perhaps the designer, too. Whoever designed the façade took as his model an engraved illustration of an Ionic temple in the Mission Library's copy of The Ten Books of Architecture by Vitruvius, a Roman architect of about the time of Christ. The four

Above: The façade of the Mission is based on an illustration of an Ionic temple by the Roman architect, Vetruvius. Right: The Crucifixion is one of the largest paintings in the California Missions. Painted in the Spanish style of religious paintings by an unknown artist.

columns in the book illustration were increased to six on the church façade, while three pedestals on top of the gable suggested the placing of the three statues of Faith, Hope and Charity, with a fourth statue of the patron, Saint Barbara, in a niche in the center. These statues, which were originally brightly painted, were carved by native Chumash artists out of local stone. These are the only such examples of monumental stone sculpture executed by native sculptors in California. Of these figures, Hope, Charity and Saint Barbara are now displayed in the Mission Museum. They were damaged in the 1915 earthquake and have been replaced by modern sculptures of the same subjects. Although the pedestals in the engraved illustrations may have suggested the placing of the virtues on the gable, the installation of similar statues atop the façade

Above: Photograph of a painting Mission Santa Barbara *(1875) by Edward Deakins. Opposite:* The Assumption and Coronation of the Virgin, *possibly a work from the Mexican studio of Miguel Cabrera in the eighteenth century, is one of the largest paintings at the Mission. It hangs to the left of the Sanctuary in the Mission Church.*

of the Mexico City cathedral during the preceding decade could have influenced the choice as well.

The combination of temple front and twin bell towers was in the latest fashion. Similar schemes can be seen in a number of contemporary churches as far apart as Baltimore, Maryland; Pamplona, Spain; and Saint Petersburg, Russia, to name only three. Thus, in spite of its isolation, Mission Santa Barbara was entirely up-to-date in its neo-classical style.

This same neo-classical style appeared in the church interior. Imitation marble was painted on the pilasters, the wainscoting and the doorframes. On the flat, plastered ceiling, carved and painted wooden designs taken from another illustration in the same volume of Vitruvius served for the attachment of a number of chandeliers. The same painted canvas altarpiece remained in use behind the altar

until it was replaced after the 1925 earthquake by another, more vividly colored design. The painted wooden statues of Saint Barbara, Saint Joseph, the Immaculate Conception, Saint Francis and Saint Dominic found on the reredos, and figures of the Holy Archangels now in the Museum, are all fine pieces which came from Mexico in the mission days.

Among the paintings of particular note now in the church are the large pictures of the Crucifixion and the Coronation of the Virgin Mary and the horizontal canvases of the Holy Archangels and of three female Franciscan saints. The Stations of the Cross are the originals that came in 1797. Such statues and paintings as these were produced in Mexico for use in the missions and other churches throughout Mexico. Other statues and painting from mission days can be seen in the Museum, along with

fine vestments, holy vessels and original furniture. Of special interest is the original tabernacle probably made by native artisans, which has pieces of abalone shell accompanying a mother-of-pearl crucifix brought from Jerusalem. Small, marbleized columns with gilded capitals, and gilded wooden rays come from a shrine for the Virgin of Sorrows which stood above the main altar until some time in the eighteen-seventies.

In front of the Mission are the handsome fountain and laundry trough with Indian-carved animals of stone as water spouts. On the hillside nearby can be seen two reservoirs (one still in use by the city), a millhouse, and a filter-house of the old water system. Farther up Mission Canyon in the Santa Barbara Botanic Garden may be seen the stone dam built in mission days. In various spots between there and the Mission, one can trace the stone channel of the aqueduct.

Above, top: The Pieta, carved of alabaster and featuring painted details, is of Spanish origin and dates from the fifteenth century. The statue was a gift to the Mission in 1928 or 1929. Left: The Madonna and Child dates from approximately 1420, and was a gift to the Mission. Right: The baptistery room in the rear of the Church.

Above: The first Mission altar and tabernacle dating from 1789, now on display in the back of the Mission Church.
Lower: The baptismal font still in use today.

ARCHITECTURE IN COLONIAL MEXICO AND ITS EFFECT ON CALIFORNIA MISSION ARCHITECTURE

Architecture in Spain was in transition at the time of the conquest of Mexico. The last of the Moors had been defeated in the same year that Columbus discovered America, but aspects of their art remained vital for another two or three centuries. Gothic architecture was reaching a glorious, if belated, flamboyant conclusion and the new Renaissance style had finally begun to arrive from Italy. Though all three styles had different decorative and architectural vocabularies, they had in common a predilection for complex and rich ornamentation so that they could easily mix and be used together. These styles were imported into the newly-conquered areas of Mexico and were soon adapted to local needs. The Spaniards found a pre-existing architectural tradition of great distinction which also had a taste for rich ornament, and they were able to adapt skills of the local tradition to their own needs. The principal innovations of the Spaniards were the introduction of true arches and vaulting over large spans and vertical interior space – features lacking in pre-Columbian architecture.

The principal structures built in the sixteenth century were churches, monasteries and related buildings, with only a small number of palaces and civic buildings. The missions built in central Mexico by the Franciscan, Dominican and Augustinian missionaries were turned into monasteries by the end of the century when their original function was exhausted. The buildings were usually of stone, often with vaulting, and the churches frequently had richly carved facades. The rather fortress-like appearance of many of them was more symbolic than functional.

In the seventeenth century, missionary activity moved to frontier areas, especially to the north. In New Mexico, a simplified version of the sixteenth century style was fused with the local Pueblo Indian architecture. Elsewhere, however, the buildings were usually a provincial version of styles in the major urban centers of Mexico. Fashions continued to come from Spain, and by the year 1600, a purer and more academic form of classicism had begun to arrive. Yet the taste for rich decoration persisted, so that the transition to the exuberant baroque style was an easy one. The seventeenth century was the period of the great cathedrals of Mexico City and Puebla and other lesser ones. The religious orders completed numerous new churches, monasteries and convents, while wealthy citizens built great palaces and haciendas.

The eighteenth century saw a continuation of the same tendencies, with even more intense ornamentation climaxing in the churrigueresque, or ultra-baroque style. A reaction to baroque excesses came in 1785 with the establishment of the Royal Academy of San Carlos in Mexico City, which had as its goal the purifying of Mexican architecture. Sent from Spain, professors of drawing and painting, printmaking, die-cutting, sculpture and architecture introduced a more sober neo-classical style. Few buildings were built in this style in central Mexico before the struggle for independence began. However, many if not most church interiors were eventually remodeled in the simpler style in the decades to come. This purer neo-classicism was the prevailing style when most of the remaining California mission buildings were constructed, which explains the Roman temple façade of the church of Mission Santa Barbara.

Opposite: The main altar in the sanctuary of the Mission Church. The reredos (canvas backdrop) displayed behind the altar has been replaced several times since the dedication of the church in 1820.

Above: The doorway to the cemetery is identified by a vanitas, or skull-and-crossbones motif, signifying death. Right: (upper) Statue of St. Francis of Assisi. (lower) El Camino Real bells were placed at each mission, with a sign indicating the distance to the next missions both north and south.